DEVOTED LOVE:

A Tribute to Couples Who Stay Together

Linda Prince Jones, Ph.D.

This book is dedicated with love to

my mother, Harriet Feldmar,

and my husband, Oliver Jones.

© 2011 Linda Prince Jones,
All Rights Reserved.

No part of this publication may be reproduced, stored in a retrieval system, or transmitted, in any form or by any means, electronic, mechanical, photocopying, recording, or otherwise, without the written permission of the author.

First published by Dog Ear Publishing
4010 W. 86th Street, Ste H
Indianapolis, IN 46268
www.dogearpublishing.net

ISBN: 978-145750-622-2

This book is printed on acid-free paper.

Printed in the United States of America

CONTENTS

ACKNOWLEDGMENTS

The best way to understand devoted love is to receive it, and my mother, Harriet Feldmar, was the most important person to teach me about devotion. She not only gave me her love, but she also provided an example of devotion in how she treated family and friends with caring, thoughtfulness, and generosity.

My husband, Oliver Jones, was the inspiration for writing this book and his devotion provided the examples that made this book possible.

Ann and George Sinkankas are friends whose contribution to our lives has gone beyond the boundaries of devotion, especially during my husband's many illnesses. They have been loyal and steadfast when we needed them the most.

I wish to thank Peg Schulte Becker for her support and suggestions throughout the process of writing this book. As a gifted artist, Peg provided inspiration and appreciation when I needed it.

Cheryl Ryerkerk helped me to believe that I could write a book, in spite of my many doubts.

There is no way of thanking all my patients and clients in person, but each one of them still lives in my mind with gratitude for letting me into their lives.

The books of Lewis B. Smedes have heavily influenced my thinking about devoted love, and I am grateful that he has written so eloquently about loyalty, gratitude, commitment, responsibility, honesty, and integrity.

INTRODUCTION

Even though devoted love is one of the most precious gifts we can give or receive, it is not easy to describe the love we feel for those who are closest to us. Often, it takes a crisis to become aware of the unique and irreplaceable bonds that we share every day. This book was written when my husband was diagnosed with kidney cancer, and I began to ponder both the gifts and the passages that forge the special union that grew within our marriage. Grief opened a series of memories that allowed me to cherish the details of our life together, images that were both common and exquisite. Writing late at night, I began to see that these details of daily living were the fragile and necessary components of devotion.

Devoted love dwells in the quiet, unobtrusive blessings that we share as a couple everyday. It is the daily habits, rituals, attitudes and choices that enrich, strengthen, and sustain love so that it is able to withstand stresses, strains, and sorrows. It is heart-driven more than passion-driven. It is fortitude not obsession; it is reliability more than drama. It is a marathon of loving not a sprint towards possession. Our small acts of today form the building blocks of tomorrow.

Devoted love is personal, profound and private. It involves being together in an exclusive, dependable, and close partnership with someone we treasure. We expose our longings and vulnerabilities, our plans and projects, our victories and defeats. It means we are able to be genuine with each other and express what is real in ourselves. When we are loved for being ourselves, flaws and all, our worthiness and value are affirmed.

Love between couples is often portrayed through the images of romance with its passion and pursuit, its longings and desires. But as romance begins to fade, a new kind of love begins to develop. Devoted love is not romance turned old and dreary; it is an on-going connection that deepens and meanders in new directions.

Devoted love entails continuity and change, clarity and confusion, harmony and discord. It is supple enough to bend with the turns and detours of living together, with problems and disappointments, conflicts and blunders. It has endured the storms of suffering and the droughts of disappointment. Its roots are deep and its branches are wide. Devoted love gives us the faith to face the future together no matter what lies ahead.

INTIMACY

Devoted love is a spacious welcoming to be ourselves when we are alone together. It is sitting side-by-side, silent and sleepy, drinking coffee from stained cups. It is bathrobe hugs, bedroom slippers, and toothpaste smiles. We put away the sterling silver, the fine china, and the fragile crystal of our public selves to relax in a nest of contentment.

We share a special affinity, a sense of communion that enables us to enter the other's world and see it from the inside. Our conversations stretch us beyond safety into the rich and tumultuous center of the person we love. When we are together it feels safe to venture into the territory of vulnerability. We are able to share what is complicated, unformed, and upsetting about ourselves.

We talk about where we are today: the obstacles, worries, and fears that are pulling us down and the ambitions, hopes, and yearnings that are pulling us forward. We share not only the headlines, but also the small print of our daily achievements and struggles.

We entrust each other with our dreams and our demons. We expose what is delicate and fragile, what no one else is meant to hear: the secrets that fill us with shame, the defeats that are too tender to disclose to others, and the mistakes that flood us with guilt. We know one another's private struggles under the smooth appearances seen by others.

An invisible current takes us beyond understanding and shapes how we respond to each other. We recognize each other's moods through the posture of confidence or the slump of defeat, through a weary smile or the sparkle of joy. We speak a secret code that recalls an adventure, a funny habit, or a conversation from the past. We communicate in gestures, glances, smiles, and touch. Intimacy means we can sit together in silence and still remain connected.

RITUALS

Devoted love flows from the steady rhythm of our connections to each other. The rituals of devoted love are like a familiar song in which we move to the music of the same melody. We have rituals of greeting and departure, of togetherness and absence, of silence and solitude, of tenderness and embracing. Over time we have adapted our ways of fitting together like a duet that harmonizes our needs together.

Rituals capture a mood that we want to hold between us. We have regular times that we set aside to be together, times to be playful and relaxed. We linger over cups of coffee; we listen to music in silence; we talk softly before falling asleep.

Rituals enhance the meaning of our relationship. They help us to live in the moment, to reflect, and to remember. They mesh our lives together after moving in separate directions during the day. Rituals create an oasis of time to enjoy each other away from the distractions, obligations, and duties of our pinched and crowded lives.

As we travel through the days and into the years, rituals give our lives a flow, a pace, and a pattern. They celebrate our history; they blend traditions of the past with the freshness of today. Rituals give us a sense of security, comfort, and belonging, of being rooted in the soil of familiarity.

ACCEPTANCE

Devoted love allows us to discover our own path, our own pace, and our own inner landscape. Devoted love is an attitude of allowing more than shaping, respecting more than restricting, tolerating more than controlling. We give each other room to develop, space to meander, and freedom to create. We travel alongside each other without imposing our own beliefs or solutions.

Giving each other space to grow is a way of loving as important as the more active forms of encouragement, support, and inspiration. We are not forced to comply with one another's wishes in order to gain affection or approval. Devoted love does not bind us with unreasonable demands or restrict us with unobtainable expectations.

The gifts of devoted love enable us to become the people we are meant to be instead of having to impress, intrigue, or entertain those who love us. Released from the images that have constrained us, we are allowed to grow the roots of our being. We learn to trust our inner visions of who we are, what we value, and where we want to go. We have more energy to devote to growth and development rather than self-protection and display.

Acceptance is more enduring than adoration, which allows no room to falter. Having to work to receive admiration means that we can topple into shame and the fear of rejection when we fail to meet each other's expectations. Acceptance is not withdrawn whenever one of us disappoints the other.

We long for acceptance of what is genuine and authentic in ourselves. We want to be known for the people we really are and be valued in spite of our faults. When we are feeling lost and empty, ashamed and afraid, devotion reminds us that we are worthy of love. Devotion during these agonizing times is a blessing beyond repayment.

GROWTH

Devoted love is a personal commitment to each other's goals, aspirations, and growth. It cultivates what is best in each of us and enables us to express our individuality, our creativity, and our resourcefulness. The freedom to discover new ideas, new talents, and new visions allows something to be born within us that did not live before.

Sometimes we need a person who can believe in our strengths before we can see them for ourselves. The tender seeds of talent require patience and protection, the warmth of encouragement, and the light of hope. Devoted love helps to keep our dreams alive. It rejuvenates what has gone stale. It energizes us and awakens a passion for living. It nourishes our imaginations, imparts a sense of vitality, and reveals possibilities.

We give each other encouragement that carries us beyond our fears of failure. When one of us stumbles, we mark the path of progress by pointing out the steppingstones instead of the slips. Devoted love helps us to see our courage when we are plagued by fear, to see our progress when we are blocked by doubt, to see our strengths when we are filled with trepidation.

25

We grow when someone believes in us when obstacles block our vision. We remind each other of the problems we have overcome, of the victories won on the brink of failure, of our triumphs over misfortune. This gives us faith to trust in our own strength and capacities.

We grow by struggling against difficulties and persevering when we want to quit. We grow by carrying the responsibilities of devotion as much as we grow from the tending and nurturing of those who love us. We grow to become the people we need to be in response to difficult circumstances.

RESPECT

Attraction provides a beginning, the motivation to move closer into trust and intimacy, but respect sustains our commitment. Respect goes beyond the heroics of a gothic novel; it is deeper than image, accomplishments, and adoration.

In devoted love, respect grows from private acts of kindness, dependability, courage, and compassion that are revealed in daily living. We respect each other's quiet virtues and decency that last through time, tension, and turmoil.

Respect affirms and strengthens what is best in each of us. It shows that we are important, that we are admired, and that we are valued. It protects our rights, enhances our dignity, and strengthens our individuality.

Respect is an invisible fence that keeps us from trespassing on one another's rights. It guards the sanctuary of individual privacy and prevents familiarity from transgressing into rudeness or possessiveness. Devoted lovers do not let the banner of "we" smash their individuality or dilute the values for which they stand. Love that is too possessive becomes root-bound, twisted, and tangled.

We uphold one another's right to live with honor, integrity, and purpose. We do not pull each other so closely that either of us feels stifled or suffocated. Unless we can be true to ourselves, love withers and dies in a heavy freeze or a scorching drought.

GENEROSITY

Generosity is love expressed in actions. It can say, "I think about you", "I miss you", "I appreciate you", and "I cherish you". It hints of romance and keeps devotion fresh and fertile. Generosity is a way of giving what matters most in a personal and gracious way. When we give generously to each other, we are giving part of ourselves and not just an item or service.

Generosity turns mundane chores into acts of devotion: giving a break from childcare, cooking a special meal, or planting a tree. Generosity comes as a surprise rather than fulfilling a request or giving a present for a ritual occasion. Generosity is inspired by kindness rather than duty, gratitude rather than debt, freedom rather than necessity.

Generosity strengthens our bond and deepens our commitment and loyalty. Love that is expressed in simple acts of caring embellishes daily living and makes us feel adored and treasured. Generosity tells of our love for each other even louder than the words that we speak.

Giving to those we love enriches our own lives. Seeing a loved one's happiness, providing relief from pain, or offering comfort when someone we love is in distress: to a generous person, giving is a grace.

GRATITUDE

Gratitude is like a photograph album of special memories. It preserves not only important occasions, but also the times when we were relaxed and carefree, laughing and playing together, and exploring new adventures. Memories, like pictures, hold life still long enough for us to savor it, to record changes, and to appreciate it.

Gratitude commemorates the special times of our lives. We see ourselves as newlyweds, young and hopeful, healthy and glowing. We see ourselves on vacation, moving into a new house, and having family celebrations. We see our children growing older, and repeating the pattern of weddings, births, and graduations.

Gratitude for our relationship deepens as we travel together. We recall all that we have received from each other, all the challenges we have faced, all that we have accomplished, and who we have become because of the journey we have shared with one another.

Gratitude shows us how devoted love grows more precious through the years. It awakens us to the blessings in our current lives and helps us to find joy in unexpected places. Gratitude inspires hope for the future. It fosters generosity.

Gratitude sustains us through losses, suffering, misfortune, and disappointments. Gratitude does not silence those longings that remain, but changes them into a search for whatever blessings we can find. It helps us to recall times of happiness even when we are deep in sorrow. Gratitude helps us to shift our vision from what we have lost to what remains to be cherished.

SORROW

Devoted love anchors us when the winds of adversity blow us off course. It provides a beam of hope through darkness. It lights the way when we are lost and sustains us when life is dismal and bleak. When we are broken and ailing, devoted love gives us the strength to keep going. Devoted love helps lift us from the pit of relentless worries, soothes our battered spirits, and instills hope when despair beckons.

When unwanted changes occur, they can destroy the hopes and dreams that give us a sense of purpose. An aching gap fills our lives when the children we desire never arrive, a chronic disease decimates our plans, or unemployment plunges us into debt and despair. There is a sour gap between what we want and how distant it seems, and we get tired of waiting.

Discouragement shows us only unsolvable problems, the pain that does not seem to get better, the loss of control. Hope can become such a part of our being that we don't recognize it as long as it is present. When hope fades, it leaves us dangling in a cold and empty void.

When darkness beckons, when our dreams are crushed, and our spirits are broken, we give each other strength and encouragement. Devoted lovers are there for each other when either of them stumbles or is crushed by fate or misfortune.

They are there even when they are depleted and overwhelmed, confounded and confused. They will we be there even when they are tired, worn out, and weak. They will do their best, even when they feel lost and bewildered by the pain that also belongs to them.

Those who love us understand our pain better than anyone else. They hear the silent words we are unable to speak, the whisper of messages beneath appearances and behavior. They sense what is unspoken and inexpressible, what may be hidden or omitted, and what is contradictory or ambiguous. Devoted lovers hear the pause of evasion, the sigh of worry, the whisper of dejection. They understand our troubles and the anguish of our losses.

LOYALTY

We are committed to facing difficulties together, standing side by side, united against intractable circumstances and capricious fate. Adversity draws us closer to each other. We ache with each other's pain, and we feel an urgent wish to help.

We become attentive when our partners are sick, compassionate when they are sad, and courageous in an emergency. Devoted love is holding hands in the doctor's office when one of us is ill; it is sharing our fears through sleepless nights; it is the ways we comfort each other through heartaches and misfortune.

Devoted love supports us when tragedy, trauma or injustice strikes. It supports us in the midst of chaos and confusion. The consistency of each other's care and loyalty during harsh times makes the world seem safer, more predictable, and less dangerous.

We help each other carry the weight of hardships by offering kindness, encouragement, inspiration, and practical advice. Devotion calls us to give our time, our attention, our energy, and our resources when someone we love is tangled in confusion, discouragement, or sorrow. Devoted couples understand that disappointments and misfortune are part of living and loving.

Trust grows from our willingness to care through life's challenges. Devoted love stirs our thoughts and concentrates them on those we love. It helps us to see more deeply, to open our hearts more widely, and to feel a more penetrating awareness of each other.

A commitment of caring runs deeper than the vows we have made or the familiar roles we perform. Devotion carries us beyond what we are required to do. We pledge all of ourselves when we are devoted; it is concern for one another's welfare in ways we cannot predict. Devoted love asks us to give when we are needed and when we have responsibilities that are ours alone.

Sometimes what is needed most is not advice but a reassuring hug, a gesture of kindness, and the willingness to be there through whatever happens. Having someone who cares nearby matters even more than the words that are spoken. Suffering can be a lonely journey, no matter how many people have walked along the path.

COOPERATION

Cooperation is like a dance in which we coordinate our movements to fit together. Sometimes one of us will lead and our complex movements will be intricately choreographed; at other times, we will function more independently, but we remain responsive, focused, and committed. Occasionally we collide with each other, pull one another in the wrong direction, or stumble over our own clumsy feet, but soon we join hands again and try to find our way back into harmony.

Sharing our hopes of today and dreams for the future, we build our plans around a common vision. We work as partners in parenting, household chores, finances, and in family, social, and community commitments. When we work as a team, our movements can flow together so seamlessly that we seem to lose the distinction between our separate selves.

As we blend our thoughts, knowledge, and observations, we pollinate each other's ideas. We compensate for each other's weaknesses; we benefit from each other's strengths. We grow from teaching each other, from listening to each other, from seeing each other's mistakes and successes.

Devoted love contains many strands woven together to form a bond that is strong yet flexible, that holds a couple together as a team, and allows each person to grow as an individual. Working together successfully increases our appreciation of one another, brings out the best in each of us, and helps to accomplish our goals more effectively.

67

FAIRNESS

With devoted love, fairness lives over time, fluctuating with the bends and turns of life. We willingly give more than our share during periods of misfortune, loss, or illness. We are influenced more by compassion than duty, gratitude more than debt.

Because partners understand each other's feelings, hopes, and struggles, fairness gleaned from caring and compassion is not the same as objective equality. Life does not place equal burdens and responsibilities in our paths, so fairness is not always found at the midpoint of compromise or at the center of equality.

The breast-feeding mother may take on greater responsibilities for a newborn baby than the father even when they are equally devoted to the child. A sick partner will not be able to carry equal responsibilities. If one partner returns to school, the financial burden may fall upon the other.

Devoted love calls us to protect and guard one another's welfare. Circumstances, skills, knowledge, or aptitude may give one partner an advantage over the other, so we do not tilt the scales of love to our own benefit. Love restrains us from exploiting one another's vulnerabilities, from imposing upon each other, and from taking more than our share.

Fairness is an intricate scale that balances our responsibilities to each other and our rights as individuals. Devoted love must be supple so we are not pulled apart by our differences or lose what makes our lives worthwhile.

Protecting something vital to one of us may mean saying "no" to the other. When this happens, we understand and respect each other's limitation and do not demand what would cost too much to give. We know that having to sacrifice too much leads to resentment rather than love.

CONFLICTS

76

Devoted love matters the most when we face each other as adversaries. Sometimes our views collide, our wills clash, our minds are set, and we block each other's movements like gridlock at rush hour.

We do not run out on each other between the fury of disagreement and the healing of forgiveness. We stay and argue; we stay and sulk; we close a door between each other. Sooner or later one of us moves towards the other circling cautiously, and gradually we touch, or smile, or make a joke that clears the stale air.

Devoted lovers remain loyal during distressing and tumultuous times because they accept the whole package of each other. Love is not a temporary feeling that disappears as soon as conflicts arise and returns only when the relationship is rewarding. We trust in the sunshine of tomorrow even during the storms and freezes of today.

Conflicts can bring us closer by clarifying misunderstandings and addressing problems before they wrench us apart. Conflicts help us to protect what is important in our relationship. Anger can be like a surgeon's blade cutting through what is false, frustrating, and unfair. Anger is often a symptom of feelings too tender and bruised to be touched by words. The more devoted we are to each other, the more we can be hurt when our partner seems to be slipping away, concealing something, or becoming distant.

Anger is like a power tool that requires great skill in handling. The force of anger can be used to benefit or to harm our relationships. Anger can cut through our problems or it can sever our fragile bond of trust. Fear can hold us back when we need to speak; anger can make us say what should be restrained.

During an argument we tend to communicate differently than in an intimate discussion. We are not so eager to understand each other as to prove our own points of view. When we change from combatants back to lovers, we try to restore our caring and closeness and seek a genuine solution to our difficulties through compromise rather than coercion.

COMMUNICATION

Sometimes our thoughts are too muddied with confusion, too mixed with pain, or too brittle with self-righteousness to speak with care and caring. The honesty we share is heavy with responsibilities. We avoid using each other's disclosures as weapons during a fight; we avoid piercing one another's dignity with judgments or shame, and we avoid revealing each other's secrets.

We wait until our words are guided by love and kindness rather than passion and impulses. We have learned to give ourselves space to reflect, to gain a better understanding, and to discover what may lie deeper inside. Patience gives us the space to explore what is complicated and confounding and keeps the process of understanding evolving.

We sense when the time is right to disclose a painful truth, to express a troubling thought, or to reveal a disturbing secret. We know when to offer encouragement, when to ask questions, and when to be silent. We see into the heart of our partner's vulnerability and know what needs protecting and what needs prodding. We see what is too painful to discuss and what needs to be shared. We see when restraint is necessary or when a difficult truth must be confronted.

The truths held by one of us affect us both. Honesty is most important when it is most difficult: when we have to tell our partners something that could induce pain, anger, or distress. It takes courage to tell the truth when it can lead to unknown changes. We need to speak of what matters and listen to what is difficult to hear. We have learned that talking honestly can shake us loose from the places in which we are stuck, and in the turmoil produced, we seek new answers to our problems.

We enlarge the opening of communication by demonstrating our willingness to travel together wherever our difficulties take us. We develop confidence in ourselves and faith in each other from challenges we have faced, from suffering we have endured, and from failures we have overcome. Our history gives us faith that we will cross the barriers of today and the hurdles of tomorrow.

TOLERANCE

Devoted love is a tender and respectful attitude towards each other's blemishes, follies, and weaknesses. It is not the wool of sentimentality, or the numbness of denial, or the pretense of excusing. Those who love us accept our quirks and foibles, our shortcomings and our flaws. They accept the whole package of our being and realize that our strengths and vulnerabilities go together to make us who we are. One of the gifts of mature love is that it allows us to be human with all our frailties and to heal our relationships even in times of discord and disappointment.

We do not give up on our relationship when lapses, messiness, or meanness slip between us. Love is not withdrawn when one of us disappoints the other, makes a mistake, or commits a transgression.
We make allowances for the ordinary misdemeanors of thoughtfulness, distraction, tactlessness, and insensitivity that cause us to clash. We do not weigh each other down with recriminations and blame.

We remember what is best about each other even during slips and blunders. We tolerate each other's bad moods and irritability and try to provide comfort and consolation. We remember each other's kindness when one of us becomes rude; we remember each other's wisdom when one of us acts foolishly; we remember each other's courage when one of us is afraid; and we remember each other's resilience when one of us seems frail.

Devoted love is not pulled away capriciously or vindictively as punishment for a wrongdoing or mistake or when life gets ugly or dreary. Those who love us do not leave when we lose contact with our better selves amid the debris of childhood feelings and adult flaws. Devoted lovers realize that they will disappoint and disturb each other.

INTEGRITY

Devoted love is not pure and untainted; sometimes it struggles against our temperaments, our tempers, and our temptations. Integrity involves loyalty in actions even when our feelings entice us toward dishonor. When we are in danger of straying from the path of courage, honesty, and fairness, self-awareness warns us before we betray our commitments to those we love.

Integrity is the moral regulator of devotion that takes control when our feelings, fears, or frustrations try to lead us into mischief. Integrity helps us confront our murky motives and devious desires without acting upon them. It helps us avoid being led astray when fascination and excitement beckon more loudly than the drudgery of duty.

Integrity awakens us when we are too tired to face what is distressing and difficult. It shows us our responsibilities and tells us when we are off track, insincere, or not in tune with our values and commitments. Integrity means remaining faithful when impulses pull us towards temptations, remaining committed when freedom is more enticing, remaining trustworthy when goals are easier to attain by bending the rules.

Integrity means the willingness to stand firmly when we want to run away; to listen when we want to retreat into denial or distractions; and to give when we are tired, tense, or intent on our own goals. Integrity is doing what is right instead of what is easy.

GUILT

Guilt fills the gap between our ideals and the tired, stressed, and irritable selves that we sometimes become. We forget something important and remember too well something petty. We speak when we should remain silent and conceal what should be shared. We brandish self-righteousness and flaunt our egos. We will be angry, short-tempered, and unreasonable. We will trespass on each other's dignity. As imperfect people, we will cause pain through our stumbling and blundering.

Guilt is more than the cold, analytical judgments of conscience; it is living with the pain of having inflicted needless suffering on those that we love. Guilt transforms their pain into our pain as well. We want to protect our loved ones from harm, including that which we ourselves unknowingly or wrongly inflict.

Guilt teaches us valuable lessons about our blind spots and biases. When we have taken our partner for granted, guilt about ingratitude teaches us to treasure our relationships more fully. When we see ourselves being rigid and self-righteous, we learn to bend more gracefully to the concerns of others. When we see how we have been selfish or stingy, we learn to give more generously.

Guilt begins the process of repentance and teaches us the value of forgiveness. Gentle remorse for our mistakes allows us to develop more honest and honorable integrity. Guilt shows us what is important, what is decent, and what is right.

Integrity develops from the ashes of our mistakes and misperceptions; it develops from our willingness to assume responsibility for both our wise and foolish decisions. The wisdom we gain from harvesting our mistakes impels us to make better choices in the future. Guilt urges us to mend and strengthen our caring for those we have hurt or neglected.

FORGIVENESS

No one can hurt us as deeply as the people we love most. The very qualities that make love so valuable also make us vulnerable to being wounded and as well as wounding, even when this is unintentional. The ways we protect ourselves may result in hurting our partners unfairly.

We want to reconnect with the people who hurt us to reclaim the caring that has been torn, broken, or lost, and heal the terrible pain that divides us. So we work to find our way back to each other through separate paths that will restore our love for one another. Even as each of us withdraws into pain too private to speak, we are brought together by the hope and faith that we can get beyond our difficulties without losing one another along the way.

We meet on different sides of forgiveness as we face the tender wounds that have been inflicted. We do not attempt to deny the seriousness of our troubles or gloss over the pain. We both seek to understand this complex and confusing predicament that has wrenched us apart.

We tell each other the truth about what happened and try to understand each other's thoughts and feelings. We clear away all that is false—the excuses, the secrets, and the denial— and face our problems with honesty. We want to repair the damage that each of us has inflicted on the other and prevent the recurrence of these mistakes and misunderstandings.

As we see each other struggling with pain and confusion, our tenderness returns. We know the secrets and shames, the scars and the blind spots that each of us holds inside. We see that the wounds that have hurt too deeply have become callused with insensitivity. We recall each other's decency, caring, and loyalty, and we are reunited with love for each other.

Forgiveness unlocks our hearts and rancor is replaced by affection. The joy of loving returns, and we appreciate what has grown between us. Forgiveness frees us from resentment of the past so our current lives are not dimmed and diminished. The bleakness of resentment sees only what is wrong, what is missing, and what is flawed, but forgiveness restores color and vitality to our relationship. We are able to appreciate the goodness of today instead of remaining trapped in bitterness and despair.

Forgiveness does not erase the pain that divided us, for that pain is written indelibly as part of our journey together. Forgiveness does not erase mistakes and regrets, but it puts them in a context that makes them more bearable. Our bond can be strengthened by this passage as we get to know each other and ourselves more deeply and realize more than ever how much we mean to each other.

COURAGE

Courage is threaded throughout devoted love. It lies in the background, silently moving through our choices and actions. Courage is not just bravery or fortitude; it is the ability to share vulnerabilities, to be honest and straightforward, to admit mistakes, and to concede to errors.

It takes courage to assume responsibility for our mistakes. It takes courage to admit our frailties and weaknesses without using them as excuses. It takes courage to face our failures without casting blame. It takes courage not to edit, flee, or obscure reality when it brings us pain. It takes courage to rebuild when our dreams crash down upon us. It takes courage to mend a broken relationship and to reach out for forgiveness.

Devoted love is not armor against pain, anguish, doubt, or fear, but it gives us the strength to endure our trials and sustain our commitments. It helps us withstand confusion and perplexity, to get lost and to keep wandering until greater clarity arrives.

Devoted love is fueled by courage that lights the way even in darkness and sustains us when life is discouraging. Courage helps us to remain devoted through the dark passageways of uncertainty, pledging to face the future together no matter what lies in our paths.

Devoted love gives us the strength to face where we are today even when we don't know what tomorrow will bring. Devoted love means living in the present instead of looking backward with regret or working incessantly to control the future. It gives us the confidence to take risks and to endure the trials of disappointment.

Devoted love accompanies us into the wilderness of uncertainty and provides a way to trust in the future and to welcome the unknown and unexpected. We have developed confidence in ourselves and faith in each other from challenges faced, from suffering endured, from disappointments overcome. The security of devoted love gives us the courage to leave the past behind and search for new opportunities. It inspires us to seek new sources of joy in unexpected places.

BIBLIOGRAPHY

Borysenko, Joan. _Guilt Is The Teacher, Love Is The Lesson._ New York: Warner Books, 1990.

Fromm, Erich. _The Art of Loving._ New York: Harper & Row, 1956.

Hargrave, Terry D. _The Essential Humility of Marriage: Honoring the Third Identity in Couples Therapy._ Phoenix: Zeig, Tucker & Theisen, 2000.

Klein, Melanie. _Envy and Gratitude & Other Works 1946-1963._ New York: Delta, 1977, London: Hogarth Press, 1975.

Lewin, Roger A. _Compassion: The Core Value that Animates Psychotherapy._ Northvale, New Jersey: Jason Aronson, 1996.

Mayeroff, Milton. _On Caring._ New York: Perrenial Library, 1972.

Ortega y Gasset, Jose. _On Love. . .Aspects of a Single Theme._ London: Jonathan Cape,1967, New York: Meridian,1957, Madrid: Revista de Occidente, 1941.

Simon, Sidney B. and Simon, Suzanne. _Forgiveness: How to make peace with your past and get on with your life._ New York: Warner Books, 1990.

Smedes, Lewis B. _Learning to Live the Love We Promise: For People Who Believe in Commitment And Wonder Why_. WaterBook, Colorado Springs, 2001._Originally published as _Caring & Commitment._ San Francisco: Harper & Row, 1998.

—. _Forgive and Forget: Healing the Hurts We Don't Deserve._ New York: Harper & Row, 1984.

—. _Mere Morality_: What God Expects from Ordinary People. Grand Rapids: William B. Eerdmans, 1983.

—. _Keeping Hope Alive: For A Tomorrow We Cannot Control._ Nashville: Thomas Nelson, 1998. Originally published: Standing on the Promises, Nashville: T.Nelson, 1998.

—. _A Pretty Good Person: What It Takes to Live with Courage, Gratitude & Integrity or When Pretty Good Is as Good as You Can Be._ San Francisco: Harper & Row, 1990.

—. *Love Within Limits: Realizing Selfless Love in a Selfish World*. Grand Rapids: William B. Eerdmans, 1978.

—. *Choices: Making Right Decisions in a Complex World*. San Francisco: Harper & Row, 1986.

Spring, Janis Abrahms with Spring, Michael. *How Can I Forgive You?: The Courage to Forgive, the Freedom Not To.* New York: HarperCollins, 2004.

Telushkin, Joseph. *Words That Hurt, Words That Heal.* New York: William Morrow, 1996.

CPSIA information can be obtained at www.ICGtesting.com
Printed in the USA
244538LV00001BA/1/P